PTSD
and Hemingway's
"A Way You'll Never Be"

The Mark of Confidence

Charles A. Coleman, Jr., Ph.D.

A PTSD PRESS MONOGRAPH

Chapel Hill   North Carolina

2014

Dedicated to

Charles A. Coleman

Russell W. Newman

William B. Stein

Credits and Copyright

Cover photo: Along the Piave River, Italy. Helen Johns Kirtland, photographer. Originally published in Leslies Weekly Newspaper. New York: Leslie-Judge Company. 1919.

Cover design, editorial assistance and graphics by Melinda Fine.

PTSD Press
ISBN-13: 978-0692232224
ISBN-10: 0692232222
LCCN: 2014910290

PTSD
and Hemingway's
"A Way You'll Never Be"

The Mark of Confidence

Ernest Hemingway described the symptoms of PTSD—and the inner workings of soldiers' minds so afflicted—decades before post traumatic stress disorder (PTSD) was recognized as a clinical condition. So striking are his depictions of "stressors" and their effects upon his protagonist that discernible "patterns of affliction" can be identified and actually tracked through the mental meanderings of Nicholas Adams in portraying situations, symptoms and manifestations of "the disorder" that mirror today's quest to better understand both PTSD and traumatic brain injury or TBI.[1,2]

Nick Adams, Hemingway's main character in his short story, "A Way You'll Never Be," appears to suffer from both PTSD and TBI (much as Hemingway may have experienced himself running ambulances out of Schio, Italy in the summer of 1918 when he was seriously wounded along the Piave River by an Austrian mortar shell).[3,4]

Far from "emotion recollected in tranquility,"[5] Nick opens the short story with the signature signs of PTSD frequently occurring with **an inventory of memorable minutia** and often catalogued in the mind of the afflicted with tedious repetition. Frequently triggered by a **stressor**, these inventories are spontaneously generated from memory, but are just as often unreliable once applied to the factual chronology of actual events.

Additionally, people suffering from PTSD create various types of cerebral **timelines**, sometimes as simple as short vignettes of loosely connected mental pictures, some with action, speech, soundtracks, words, and associated odors. But these timelines are really just disconnected snippets of memories and not always accurate nor sequential and so do not conform to the more traditional definition of timeline as a way of describing and displaying a list of events in a strict chronological sequence or order. Timelines, along which key events are posted, are sometimes referred to as **project artifacts** ("using art" + "something made") in which events and milestones are highlighted and enumerated in a graphic design displayed along a time bar.

Nicholas Adams begins stockpiling his memorable minutia with his inventories of the dead and their associated artifacts starting with "papers" and "paper" (at the end of the second paragraph) that are repeated in each of the two following paragraphs intermixed with "postcards," "cards," "photographs," "pictures," and "the letters, letters, letters" of the dead.

> There was always so much paper about the dead and the debris of this attack was no exception.

These graphic images are artifacts in their own right: "period pieces," in some cases "just the occasional pictures of children," others are "small photographs of village children by village photographers" and still others are scattered with "the smutty postcards, photographic." The reflections and refractions of looking at the minutia of the dead are captured through various lenses of perspective through Hemingway's literary camera and rendered in this awesome deathscape punctuated by the repetition of the minutia:

> . . . many of the calfskin-covered haversacks, stick bombs, helmets, rifles, . . . the bayonet stuck in the dirt . . . stick bombs, helmets and rifles, entrenching tools. . .

ammunition boxes . . . full belts protruding from the boxes
. . . and around them, in the grass, more of the typical
papers.

Nowhere are the physical characteristics of the dead
themselves described, except for the mention of their "positions"
and that "the hot weather had swollen them all alike regardless of
nationality."

The dead are faceless, nameless and in fact barely make it into
the catalogue of Nick's re-collected "artifacts." But the setting is
vibrant, searing, and memorable which in turn causes Nick to
reconstruct what he remembers of what happened during the
Austrian assault on the village.

This, the first of many **flashbacks** (beginning with the seventh
paragraph), initiates what becomes a repetitious, haunting and
evasive thread of **contested authenticity** of Nick's memory of the
topographical attributes of this section of the Paive River, the
landmarks of trees and houses along its banks, and his personal
involvement as a person in this place and in this time, past and
present, and—as we'll see—future.

Hemingway tips his hand to the importance of this memorable
re-collection and its impact on Nick when he describes the
Austrian position through Nick's eyes:

> It was all very lush and over-green since he had seen it last
> and becoming historical had made no change in this, the
> lower river.

This "**becoming historical**" is a remarkably insightful
interpretation of what goes on in re-collective thought processes of
people afflicted with traumatic stress. It is precisely here, in
"becoming historical," that the **three primary points of the
triangle-of-self become self-evident: Time. Space. Place**. This

forms the basis of "history" as the knowledge of objects determined by space and time as provided by memory. Nick struggles to get the actual sequence of his history of events "right" along a timeline that "makes sense" so that he has some **mark of confidence** in his memory and the way he fits into them. This drive to "get it right"—so that the individual can adapt to a rational history of what "was" and therefore presumably serve as a platform for what "is" when transitioning out of being held hostage by the whims of memory rooted in fear, horror, guilt and self-destructiveness—is a critical driver in the psychological functioning of those suffering from PTSD.

In essence, Nick is testing the authenticity of his story and his own personal history with respect to the landmarks, objects, and topographical features of this section of the Piave River, the lower river.

It's as though he's holding up two negatives: one a photo of what the past landscape looked like (as an "old" artifact stored in his memory), and the other of the photo he is just now taking through his eye and then superimposing one over the other. The "test" is how closely they resemble each other, how closely they "match:" indeed, in this case, the match is so close that Nick sees no need to alter the way he remembers the past landscape with his current "snapshot." There is no need for anxiety since all is "familiar."

For people suffering from PTSD, **semblance, resemblance, identity, recall and memory** are all so intimately interdependent as part of our cognitive functioning that even a single episode of failure among them can cause a breakdown in the individual's confidence of his own state of mind and therefore a radical displacement of his very identity. When a break occurs, it often manifests itself in self-doubt and frustration leading to rage, fear, violence, paranoia, and other neurotic and psychotic behaviors that we have come to associate with the symptoms of PTSD.[6]

For Nick, this first "test" along the "lower river" does not challenge the accuracy of his recollection and therefore does not undermine his sense of self. There are no "dissenting voices," if you will, with which he has to contend at the moment; but he does have to deal with an abrupt issue of his **identity** when a "young second lieutenant with a stubble of beard and red-rimmed, very bloodshot eyes pointed a pistol at him" and asks:

"Who are you?"

Nick explains who he is, but the lieutenant wants proof. So what does Nick do? He produces a "tessera" with a photograph of himself, and identification, and the Seal of the Third Army. A tessera, in this context, is an identification card and military pass, the same sort of "card" with a photograph that Nick has catalogued among the minutia of the dead. The lieutenant challenges Nick yet again:

"How am I to know who you are?"

The lieutenant is still distrustful. Not even with a photograph can the lieutenant be certain of Nick's identity and so Nick speaks for his tessera:

"The tessera tells you."
"And if the tessera is false?"

The issue of Nick's identity is raised almost immediately again when this same lieutenant brings Nick face-to-face with the commander of the battalion, Captain Paravicini, but not before Hemingway interposes a scene meant to hint at future dislocations and confusions in Nick's mind with respect to mixing up people, places, events and time:

As Nick had left the edge of the town three shrapnel had burst high and to the right over one of the wrecked homes and since then there had been no shelling. But the face of this officer looked like the face of a man during a bombardment.

Hemingway has ever so slightly planted the seed of doubt in both the reader's mind (and Nick's) as to Nick's reliability as a credible "witness" when telling his story (history), which gets played out in greater detail as the story progresses.

Now for the meeting between Captain Paravicini and Nick at the battalion headquarters: Nick is at first relieved to know that "Para" is still alive and apparently in control of the battalion. We get the feeling that Para will instantly establish Nick's identity once and for all since Para and Nick apparently know each other, Nick likely having served under his command in some capacity. Hemingway stages the reunion in such a way that, for a split second, challenges Nick's identity yet again:

> The Captain Paravicini, acting major, thinner and more English-looking than ever, rose when Nick saluted from behind the table. . . .
> "Hello," he said. "I didn't know you. What are you doing in that uniform?"

To which Nick replies:

> "They put me in it."

Nick is now the Universal Soldier. Here, identity suddenly becomes multifaceted: no longer is it just about recognizing the individual as a person remembered, but now identity is determined by the uniform which speaks more to the identity of the uniform than the man wearing it. This is essentially what Nick is saying when he replies, "They put me in it."

For many vets, being in uniform on active duty one day and discharged wearing civilian clothes the next is all but mindwrenching. As one (now homeless) vet said:

> "In uniform, you're somebody. Your name's printed on your breast pocket. You have a rank. You have a patch that tells the world what Unit you belong to. You know who to salute and who not to. What theaters and battles you've been in. If you've been wounded. Decorated. In civilian clothes, you're a Nobody. I'm a No-body."[7] (Oddly, within the next few paragraphs, the issue of "uniforms" and clothing is raised by Para.)

Nick's apparently been stripped of his Italian Army uniform and made to wear another: a makeshift American uniform. "They" have not only put Nick in another uniform and given him a new identity, but "they" have apparently sent him back to the front lines with a new mission where he's "supposed to move around and let them [the Italian soldiers] see the uniform." To which Para replies:

> "I'm sure your appearance will be very heartening to the troops."

Para's statement is a subtle reference that whatever happened to Nick will not go unnoticed by the troops who will be heartened at seeing that Nick has recovered and seems fine. That Para has knowledge of this "something" and how it relates to Nick's new identity and role is alluded to in the sentence about "appearance."

To which Nick replies:

> "I wish you wouldn't. I feel badly enough about it as it is."

This is perhaps the first acknowledgement that there's something about Nick's past that's bothering him to the extent that he feels guilty and defensive for something that he's done, or something in which he was involved, or something that was done to him.

When Nick says, "I wish you wouldn't," it leaves the reader asking, "wouldn't what?" The question is amplified by Nick's next statement that: "I feel badly enough about it as it is." What is the "it" to which he is referring?

This begins a chorus of "its" that reverberates throughout the rest of the story, literally to the last page. As it turns out, the "it" is many things, but all related to Nick and his psychological and physiological trauma and his lack of confidence in his sanity and therefore his identity, his inner sense of self. He faces the fact that he may not be able to trust himself to be himself any longer and it frightens him.

Para soon begins to unravel the nature of the mystery and helps us to piece together some of the major "its," beginning by offering Nick some Grappa (which some troops drank with rum and ether)[8] and mentioning that

> "It hasn't any ether in it."

The reference to ether triggers an immediate reaction from Nick:

> "I can taste that still," Nick remembered suddenly and completely.

Indeed, taste and smell are two of the most powerful triggers of memory. Recollections "fired" by the senses are "transporters," instantly connecting past sensations and memories with the present. In this case, though, the mention of ether doesn't immediately trigger a flashback but rather an acknowledgement that the memories associated with his experience with ether are closer to the surface of consciousness than he might have thought. These memories are "top of mind:" the taste of ether (which we must suspect was used as an anesthetic on Nick) is the first hint that he was wounded and probably required surgery.

The mention of Grappa and the effects of ether propel the conversation into an exchange about states of drunkenness before, during and after the major attacks in which both Nick and Para participated, Para claiming that he hadn't seen Nick drunk before or during any attack while Nick rebuts that he was "stinking in every attack." This "conversation" is ended abruptly by Nick when he says:

> "Let's not talk about how I am," Nick said. "It's a subject I know too much about to want to think about it any more."

Here, the "it" is specifically Nick, and more specifically the subject of "how I am." Nick's reaction to Para's probing into Nick's states of drunkenness "in the lines" provokes his response (above) and is typical of many individuals suffering from PTSD— the classic approach-avoidance paradox. Nick can go along with the flow of the conversation—and Para's observations of Nick—up until that point when Nick feels uncomfortable discussing "it" any further. And yet, for many people who have experienced post-traumatic stress, there's always this tension, a kind of mental tug-o-war of <u>wanting to</u> talk about the traumatic events, the stressors, the memories, and the effects on that person and <u>not wanting to</u> disclose or to verbalize anything beyond a certain point.

But Para changes his indirect approach to evaluating Nick's condition and comes right out and challenges Nick with:

> "How are you really?"

To which Nick replies:

"I'm fine. I'm perfectly all right."

But Para persists, much like the second lieutenant who initially challenged Nick's identity:

"No. I mean really."

Nick "gives up" the fact that:

"I'm all right. I can't sleep without a light of some sort. That's all I have now."

The issue about why Nick now can't sleep without a light on is as important to understanding his mental state as:

"That's all I have now."

What Nick's admitting is that he's as uncertain of his current condition ("now") as his future condition. The only aftereffect of his experiences is the need now to have a light on when he tries to fall asleep. It's as if he's trying to confine his condition to that one change, as though that's the only thing wrong with him. Nick only mentions this external change in behavior (i.e. the dependency on the light when trying to fall asleep) while not revealing the cause, which triggers an assumption when Para says:

"I said it should have been trepanned. I'm no doctor but I know that."

This statement leaves little doubt that Nick has experienced some sort of trauma to the head and therefore to his brain (i.e. potential TBI), likely a concussion caused by an incoming mortar blast, "one of those big noises you sometimes hear at the front."[9] Also, "it" takes on yet another meaning personal to Nick: his skull and his brain.

Para thinks that the doctors should have drilled a hole (trepan) in Nick's skull to alleviate the swelling from the likely concussion, but apparently they chose another option according to Nick:

> "Well, they thought it was better to have it absorb, and that's what I got. What's the matter? I don't seem crazy to you, do I?"

Whatever psychological event Nick lived through, he also has a physical injury which he fears may affect his mental functioning to the point of doubting his own sanity. Note that the "it" in "better to have it absorb" is now used to refer to Nick's brain.

That Nick has to ask Para if he appears crazy sets Nick up for the rest of the story, but with the lingering doubt about what Para says in response:

> "You seem in top-hole shape."

"Top-hole" is a British colloquialism meaning "first-rate, excellent," but it seems that Para is using the expression here to suggest that Nick has recovered just as well as if he had been trepanned, since Para thinks that was the appropriate procedure, hence "top-hole."

Nick is still fixated on the notion that he may be crazy when he says:

> "It's a hell of a nuisance once they've had you certified as nutty. No one has any confidence in you again."

Here, the "it" is having been certified as nutty, or crazy, or insane by "they," presumably a military (Italian Army?) medical board.

The stigma—and the fact that "no one has any confidence in you again"—are two of the primary external and internal determinants that affect the behavior of anyone trying to avert "the label."[10] Nick is clearly sensitive to this, maybe even paranoid as evidenced by his anxiety and withdrawal from the troops who were in the same room while he "napped." As he lies down on the bunk to which Para points him, Hemingway commences with an internal monologue in Nick's mind that starts with confirming one of Nick's greatest fears.

> Nick lay on the bunk. He was very disappointed that he felt this way and more disappointed even, that it was so obvious to Captain Paravicini.

Note again the "it." What Nick earmarks as so "obvious" is Nick's projection of his sense of his "condition" onto the observer, in this case Para. The "it" has created the "disappoint," and now refers to him being potentially "nutty." The real take-away from these two lines is—for sufferers of PTSD and TBI—that it's not so much about disappointing "the other," but the rather the disappointment the self feels. The external projection becomes a reflection of the internal doubts, apprehensions, fears, guilt and shame of not being "normal" anymore: "Mirror, mirror on the wall. Who is the craziest of them all? Me," one vet recalled while shaving.[11]

Then, oddly, for nearly two pages without a break, Nick's consciousness bobs and weaves from third person, to first, to second in a mishmash of what reads like free associative run-on sentences and images where time, space, person, place, and events are all jumbled up into what reads like the meanderings of a madman.

And yet, of course, they're not. Hemingway makes a subtle but important distinction between stream of consciousness and free- or random-association of thought, and that distinction is crucial to understanding the thought processes of those afflicted with PTSD and/or TBI and, further, the distinction between a daydream, a nightdream and a nightmare.

The fact that much of this story-as-flashback takes place along a river reflects the author's use of stream of consciousness narrative techniques. It is a narrative device used to "depict the multitudinous thoughts and feelings which pass through the mind." The term **"stream of consciousness"** was first coined in 1890 by psychologist William James in his *The Principles of Psychology* where he defines it as such:

> consciousness, then, does not appear to itself as chopped up in bits. . . it is nothing joined; it flows. A 'river' or a 'stream' are the metaphors by which it is most naturally described. In talking of it hereafter, let's call it the stream of thought, consciousness, or subjective life.[12]

This "it" above is precisely what transpires in Nick's mind for well over two pages in the first sequence and then verbalized in a slew of run-on sentences in the second sequence lasting for a page and a half. Note that in the above definition of "stream of consciousness" that consciousness "does not appear **to itself** chopped up in bits." Perhaps to an outsider listening to a verbalization of an individual's stream of consciousness thoughts the representation of consciousness may appear to be "chopped up in bits," but to the consciousness belonging to the individual it does not appear to be chopped up into bits at all.

Note also that James acknowledges straight away that "it" is a "subjective life." Indeed, much of the struggle for those afflicted with PTSD is exactly that, sorting out the "subjective life" of their memories of the past that impinge on both the accuracy of those recollections as well as the harsh realities of today, which may include joblessness, failed relationship(s), impotence, bouts of uncontrollable anger, crippling paranoia, hypervigilance, divorce, aggressive arousal, restraining orders, forgetfulness, reckless behavior, drug and alcohol dependencies, jail time and suicide.

In this first sequence, after Nick agrees to lie down on the bunk, the first thought that comes into his mind is his sense of disappointment in himself "that was so obvious" to Para. In the sequences that follow, overflowing with images and snapshots rich in preparing for the battlefield, this stream of consciousness completely breaks down into a mishmash of pronouns running the gambit from "he" to "I" to "we" to "them" to "my" to "his," etc. until Nick runs head on into a series of associations and memories that well up and frighten him beginning with:

> Sometimes his girl was there and sometimes she was with someone else and he **could** not understand that, but those were the nights that the river ran so much wider and stiller than it **should**. . . [Emphasis mine.]

It would appear that we are back to third person omniscient as Hemingway begins "undermining" Nick's internal credibility again with "he could not understand that," i.e. that fact that "his girl" is "there . . . with someone else," suggesting that she isn't as much "his girl" as he would have thought. Connected to this alteration is the fact that "his girl" being with him or someone else occurs concurrently with nights when "the river ran so much wider and stiller than it should."

This first sequence of "internal monologue" contains more (at least six) of the three auxiliary verbs (should, would, could) than anywhere else in the story, and this first sentence (above) is a good example of how "could" and "should" are used to confound tenses and therefore timelines as Nick's artifacts get jumbled up in his stream of consciousness. W*ould, should* and *could* can be defined as the past tenses of *will, shall*, and *can* respectively. They can also be used to suggest conditionality, all of which are based on timelines and the causal relationships among the artifacts.

Note also that the first formal tone of anthropomorphism is introduced in this passage by Nick via the author bestowing human aspects of conscious behavior on to an inanimate object, in this case the river. Nick's assertion of the river's characteristics or "behavior" as being "so much wider and stiller than it should be" suggest that the river is somehow responsible for being wider and stiller than Nick thinks it "should" be. The sense here is that Nick is feeling threatened by "those. . . nights" when the river was not as it should be and "his girl" is not with him but rather "with someone else" and has associated the river and its width as the cause of his anxiety.

This is the ripple effect of these waves of consciousness crashing over Nick's recollections and undermines his own sense of confidence in his own memories and therefore his very sanity. Beginning with this inability to "understand that" as the antecedent thought to the river being other "than it should be" infuses his memories with a foreboding sense of uneasiness that accentuates Nick's uncanny dissemblance of the way he recalls the upcoming, critical topology of the river, the house, the stable, the canal, the hill and the boat:

> . . . outside of Fossalta there was a low house painted yellow with willows all around **it** and a low stable and there was a canal, and he had been there a thousand times and had never seen **it**, but there **it** was every night as plain as the hill, only **it** frightened him. [Emphasis mine.]

Here, as Nick once again takes inventory of what would appear to be a recognizable topology, the "its" are back in abundance! Thus begins Nick's latest catalogue of what he recalls from his past juxtaposed against a more recent "visit" to the same location in his dreamscape. "It" expands in meaning in Nick's mind from just a "low house painted yellow" to something he "had never seen" to something that in fact had been there "every night as plain as the hill," to something that "frightened him."

To what does the last "it" (above) refer? On the surface, it could simply be the house, but in fact there's a more insidious, debilitating threat emerging and that's Nick's recognition that his memory is faulty and therefore his mind is untrustworthy, both of which challenge his rational being.

Here again, the overlay of the two topographical "photographs" developed in the darkroom of the mind is contrasted in the litmus test of "sameness" that proved to be acceptable and therefore became "historical" in the light of day earlier in the morning when "It was all very lush and over-green since he had seen it last and becoming historical had made no change in this, the lower river." That is clearly **not** the case here. There is no confirmation of likeness, or semblance or similarity. We are now in another situation altogether, and Nick is scared. But of what, exactly? Based upon what we now know of how Hemingway is depicting the signs and symptoms of what would be called post-traumatic stress disorder and/or traumatic brain injury, it's clearly the threat that Nick senses about his inability to "get it right," and to have confidence in his remembrances of things past, all dependent on his notion of a "thing:" in this case a house.

> That house meant more than anything and every night he had it.

"That house" has become a complex icon among the artifacts in Nick's collection: complex, critical, and essential to his identity. It's his spiritual rallying point. A stake in the ground in the landscape of his consciousness, and the cornerstone of what holds him together at this moment in his internal remembrances of what was. It's like the reassurance we feel when we're "at home" with our surroundings: familiar, known, secure.

Auguste Comte remarked that mental equilibrium

was, first and foremost, due to the fact that the physical objects of our daily contact change little or not at all, providing us with an **image of permanence and stability**. They give us a **feeling of order** and tranquility. . . . In truth, much mental illness is accompanied by **a breakdown of contact between thought and things**, as it were, an inability to recognize familiar objects, so that the victim finds himself in a **fluid and strange environment totally lacking familiar reference points**. So true is it that our habitual images of the external world are inseparable from our self that this breakdown is not limited to the mentally ill. We ourselves may experience a similar period of uncertainty, **as if we had left behind our whole personality**, when we are obliged to move to novel surroundings and have not yet adapted to them.[13] [Emphasis mine.]

Exactly: Nick suddenly finds himself on a very slippery slope when associating emotions with physical landmarks in the line of sight of his stream of consciousness, especially during the "breakdown between thought and things." Indeed, this is the point of no return for Nick, because once he crosses this line in his cortex of what was and what wasn't will determine whether or not he can regain his mental equilibrium and that "mark of confidence" he so desperately needs to survive.

With the generation of "that house," Hemingway creates a profound juxtaposition, really a catastrophic collision, among the remembrances of the arrangements of those things so critical to Nick's own sense of sanity. This is the point where—unlike in the previous revisiting of a landmark (e.g. "the lower river") which was benignly "**becoming historical**"—Nick is on a trajectory to **becoming hysterical**.

> . . . a low house painted yellow. . . it frightened him. That house meant more [to him] than anything and every night he had it. That is what he needed but it frightened him
> . . . .

That which "he needed," that which "meant more than anything," and that "it" which "he had" all seem to conspire ("it") to frighten him. By conjuring these associations with "that house," specifically with what "he had," sets Nick up for a catastrophic loss. Once upon a time—at least in his mind—he had something to "have and to hold," something he owned, had possession of, and that which he could recognize in memory and rely upon as a waypoint on his journeys through his past. But once that is lost, destroyed, challenged, or overshadowed with fear and loathing, Nick is screwed. One could also make the association of "that house" with the earlier seen of foreboding when Nick is feeling threatened by "those. . . nights" when the river was not as it should be and "his girl" is not with him but rather "with someone else."

Nick is justifiably frightened: he could lose his bearings, his identity, his sanity and his self if he cannot rationally come to terms with his "condition." Nick is clearly out of his "comfort zone" now, and has entered into a psychological topology of recollection that causes him great discomfort, uneasiness, and an uncanny sensation of not-being-at-home with what he recalls of where he was, what he was doing, and who he was. Nick's sense of "uncanniness" is what Martin Heidegger describes as *Unheimlichkeit*,[14] that sensation of "not-being at-home," of an angst that something about my surroundings isn't right as our world begins to falter and our mental home crumbles. Some things are out of time and out of place, or misplaced, or "just not right" with our Self.[15]

Becoming hysterical: Hysteria has had a long and rather colorful evolution in psychology and psychiatry,[16] but regardless of how hysteria is or is no longer defined, the manifestation of hysteria is something abnormal by any definition in that dissociative disorders involve disruptions, interruptions, and breakdowns of memory, awareness, or perception—"**nutty**," to quote Nick, or "dotty" to quote the patients once housed in a not-quite-forgotten British Army mental hospital (Craiglockhart)[17] recovering from a variety of "mental problems," including "trench trauma" and shell shock, possible precursors to TBI and/or PTSD.

Here again Nick is experiencing severe dislocations of time, place and space and mixes up people, events and chronology in the midst of his daydream as "that house" emerges as a metaphor for his elusive mark of confidence, a litmus test of sanity:

> . . . but it frightened him especially when the boat lay there quietly in the willows on the canal, but the banks weren't like this river.[18]

"This river." The Paive River? Or "lower" . . .

> . . . as it was at Portogrande, where they had seen them come wallowing across the flooded ground holding their rifles high until they fell in the water. Who ordered that one?

Which is fiction and which is fact in Nick's account? Or are they all "factual" but just all mixed up?[19]

Confounding is a signature symptom of those suffering from PTSD, regardless of severity, and is sometimes confused with prevaricating: "Those damn vets. Lying all the time."[20] As a transitive verb, confound means to cause to become confused or perplexed; to fail to distinguish between two or more subjects or objects; to mix up; to make something bad even worse; to frustrate, obfuscate, or derail. But to those suffering from PTSD, they don't see themselves as liars at all: they are telling the truth as they know it regardless of how inaccurate or dissembling **it** may be.

Nick's confounding has confounded his Self, in all aspects of the word. Not only is he confounded, he's compromised, with his mark of confidence now more on the line than ever before.

> If it didn't get so damned mixed up he could follow it all right. That was why he noticed everything in such detail to keep it all straight so he would know where he was, but suddenly it confused without reason as now, he lying in a bunk at battalion headquarters, with Para commanding a battalion and he in a bloody American uniform.

Here we are full circle with the "its"—the curation of the detailed minutia of memorabilia, the mix up of the artifacts on the timelines, the conditional "would," the incessant obsession to "get it right" and "keep it all straight so he would know where he was," his identify crisis amplified by "he lying . . . in a bloody American uniform"—all of which is brilliantly summed up in the phrase

> . . . suddenly it confused without reason as now. . . .

Here Hemingway shows his hand again in drawing our attention to Nick's mental disintegration "without reason," a figure of speech that usually equates to that which is illogical, irrational, abrupt, unnecessary, unprompted, and sometimes "out of character." (Note that Hemingway cuts to the chase and resists the cliché, "without rhyme or reason," although in so doing he again amplifies the discordance in Nick's mind—there is no rhyme, no correspondence, no reciprocating echo in thought, imagery and inner speech, no metrical structure.)

In pointing to the "it" in the phrase above, Hemingway is begging the questions: what specifically is the "it" that in turn has "confused" what? By this point in the story, we already have a pretty good idea about this "it" and that "what." Nick's mental health is collapsing into chaos before our very eyes with an eeriness that could likely be described as a nervous breakdown, in this case an acute displacement of our protagonist in terms of a time-bound "neurotic episode." The "it" is the disruptive invasion into his "mental equilibrium" causing a topo-logical warp between connectedness, continuity and boundaries of person, place, time, space and artifact or, to put "it" into a more clichéd phrase, the antithesis of "a place for everything and everything in its place:"

> That was why he noticed everything and in such detail to keep it all straight so he would know just where he was. . . .

Sufferers of PTSD often fall into this quagmire of micro-analysis of their past experiences. It turns into a spiraling, repetitive collection of minutia, of detail that often descends into frustration and later to despair with their inability to rise above it all and to see the forest through the trees.

Nick is likely now somewhere between Scylla and Charybdis. Now everything is suddenly displaced. Any sense of a timeline—or lifeline—is lost. He can no longer triangulate his current position or course forward, no more dead reckoning, no more compass or rhumb lines, no mental bearings to his must-have landmark (the "yellow house"). His ship of mental stability, his mark of confidence is going down: hence, the paralytic, trance-like nature of his dissociative state.

This is so remarkably typical of individuals afflicted with PTSD that it stands out front and center: navigation through the icons of memory is often a difficult and perilous journey. Nick desperately needs to "keep it all straight so he would know just where he was." Time and the artifacts of recollection and linearity now become the critical factors in Nick's ability—or in this case his foreboding inability—to establish his whereabouts and his position by ordering and sequencing events, landmarks, time and place. Of note is that Hemingway once again uses "would" as a past tense of "will," but it could also be a conditional construct as well, as in "if he could keep it all straight, then he would know just where he was."

These are the last thoughts that Nick has as he opens his eyes, momentarily, to see "they [are] all watching him." Are all of them really watching him? Or is this simply the classical, paranoid reaction of a man who knows he's in the throes of losing his mind?

Nick lies down again, but the lack of synchronization with Time has undermined all sense of chronology and the ordering of the artifacts which, fortunately for Nick, he is aware of when he "restarts" his stream of consciousness thought process with

> The Paris part came earlier. . . .

But what looks like the first attempt to bring some order ("The Paris part") to his chaos of consciousness (and perhaps even sub-consciousness) and the fact that he "was not frightened by it" turns out to be a false start on numerous fronts but none more conflicted and potentially dissembling as the catalogue of jarringly dissimilar snapshots of the same scenes of a long, low yellow house on the banks of a river of varying widths.

> Now he was back here at the river, he had gone through that same town, and there was no house. Nor was the river that way.

Think back to the litmus test of his sanity, that "mark of confidence" Nick established early on when

> It was all very lush and over-green since he had seen it last and becoming historical had made no change in this, the lower river.

Nick is lost among the ruins of his mind, overwhelmed by remembrances of a dislocated past associated with repetitive but eerily conflicting landmarks, scenes, events and emotions of fear that plague every conscious step he tries to take to try to piece together his past and therefore his identity: Who am I? What did I do? Where am I? Where was I? Where will I be transported next? . . . . Terrorizing!

Nick has completely lost control of his ability to think rationally, or as Hemingway has said, he is being subjected to forces "without reason." Sufferers of PTSD often recount numerous panic-stricken episodes such as Nick's when they feel so outrun and overtaken by repetitive but disjunctive memories both on and off the field of battle that they experience a kind of dissociation or fugue-like state. Most clinicians would agree that it's a mechanism for distancing oneself (or Selfs) from a particularly stressful, harrowing, frightening, or painful recollection that can lead to serious depression, violent behavior, and suicide.

As one veteran said:

> "I feel like Humpty Dumpty. Once fallen, I could never muster enough to put my Self back together again. Everything is broken. I thumb through family albums of my Self and my sisters and parents and it makes no sense. Everything I enjoyed about life and my relationships are nothing more than broken toys in the attic. It is a dusty, suffocating heap of shattered dreams. And lost journeys full of broken promises you made to your Self before you fell."[21]

Nick, in a state of complete dislocation, suddenly faces the ultimate memory fault line when the author poses the challenge to Nick's anxiety-inducing mental meanderings as he seemingly steps outside of himself:

> Then where did he go each night and what was the peril and why would he wake, soaking wet, more frightened than

he had ever been in a bombardment, because of a house and a long stable and a canal?

Nick is apparently unable to recall or reconnoiter his location and his actions that are connected to his potential exposure to risk of harm or loss: indeed, at this point Nick has lost his mind and he senses his vulnerability.

Suddenly, Nick is awake and aware of the specific people in the room staring at him and then, for some reason, he puts on his helmet and starts running on about what he perceived his mission to be: handing out chocolate, postcards, and cigarettes. But without these "hand outs," Nick defaults back to "the uniform" to reestablish his identity even though Nick is quick to point out that "the uniform is not very correct." Not even the uniform—the outward facing manifestation of a soldier and his "fall back" identity—is accurately rendered. Nick is neither fish nor fowl and responds defensively:

> "But it gives you the idea. There will be several million Americans here shortly."

In the next passage, Nick plunges headlong in a typical PTSD rant of self-deprecating juxtapositions in which he contrasts what he isn't to what he catalogues as the attributes of the "typical" American soldier.

There are two primary types of self-deprecating behaviors among those suffering from PTSD: the first type is a comparison between who the individual was prior to the events and stressors that lead up to the symptoms of PTSD versus who that individual is today: a before and after snapshot of him or her. The disparagement of one's Self calls attention to the individual's physical appearance and prowess before-and-after; or he might belittle aspects of himself (personality, furtive behavior, stuttering, rambling on, moral and ethical pronouncements, etc.) that he feels are "abnormal," and "even frighteningly repulsive," as one veteran described himself.[22] This type of self-disparagement is usually confined to the differences before-and-after of the same individual often envisioned as two different people: Me(1) and Me(2), or even multiples thereof (multiple personalities).

The second type of self-deprecation is the intentional degradation of the individual by comparing his or her deficiencies and limitations to a well-defined cohort of "others." It is a private "statement" of internal negativism made public by comparing and contrasting the individual to an externalized reference group: in this case it's "a me" and "a them." It's a way of making the individual small, immaterial and deficient while elevating key, positive aspects of the reference group soon leading to another episode in which Nick becomes hysterical.

The latter is Nick's method of self-deprecation, notably when he responds to the adjutant's question:

> "Do you think they will send Americans down here?"

To which Nick replies:

> "Oh, absolutely, Americans twice as large as myself, healthy, with clean hearts, sleep at night, never been wounded, never been blown up, never had their heads caved in, never been scared, don't drink, faithful to the girls they left behind them, many of them never had the crabs, wonderful chaps. You'll see."

Nick, in describing all these positive attributes of the idealized American soldiers, is highlighting what he thinks or feels he is not, hence his fall from innocence and resultant "inferiority complex" laced with guilt and shame. But even with such a blatant, soul-bearing personal contrast with his "model" American troops, the adjutant takes Nick to his knees when he asks:

"Are you an Italian?"

Again, the outward signs and symbols of who Nick is (to the "viewing public") are so inauthentic and conflicting that no one can really tell who or what he is:

"No, American. Look at the uniform."

Nick tries to set the record straight once again by acknowledging that his uniform is "not quite correct," but even that provokes yet another inquiry into his identity by the adjutant:

"A North or South American?"
"North," Nick said. He felt **it** coming on now. He would quiet down. [Emphasis mine.]

The "it" is the accumulated sum-total of everything wrong with Nick and everything that is wrong with the world he finds himself inhabiting: the fight-or-flight mentality of dealing with conflict, both inwardly and outwardly, is about to get played out again as he senses **it** coming on.

He's challenged by the adjutant yet again:

"But you speak Italian."

Nick replies—and one would have to assume not in a "quiet down" tone of voice—

"Why not? Do you mind if I speak Italian? Haven't I a right to speak Italian?"

The challenges to Nick's identity continue as he tries to explain the ribbons, and "the paper" and the medals as Nick starts the first of the dislocated verbal meanderings that comes roaring to the forefront a few paragraphs later. But what's most illuminating about this back-and-forth with the adjutant is Nick's pronouncement:

"But now I am reformed out of the war."

"Reformed" is a loaded word, and the way in which Hemingway has devised the structure of the sentence lends a critical insight into the mind of his character as Nick tries again to "explain" himself. "Reformed" can mean to form again (re-form) or to take shape in a new configuration, but it can also be used as an adjective to describe someone or something that has undergone a change or transformation, such as "a reformed alcoholic."

"But why are you here now?"

Now that's the million dollar question: why is Nick "here" in the first place? The irony of course is Nick's answer to the adjutant:

"I am demonstrating the American uniform," Nick said. "Don't you think **it** is very significant?" [Emphasis mine.]

"Demonstrating" means to clearly show the existence of the truth of something by giving proof or evidence, but Nick's uniform is so clearly a bastardization of the American uniform that not even he can concede that it resembles an American uniform, perhaps because it was made by an Italian (Spagnolini) and because it is "not very correct." In this uniform, since it is essentially a fraud of some sort, Nick feels like an imposter somehow carrying out a fraudulent mission, perhaps one he concocted all on his own since he has no "chocolate, postal cards and cigarettes" to give away and is wearing Italian ribbons:

"I am, however, wearing the uniform."

It's as though Nick's in a state of morphing from one form into another that's as yet unfinished, even as he describes the uniform as a "little tight in the collar" and perhaps he's "between sixes and sevens" when he connects the American uniform with the impending arrival of "untold millions wearing this uniform swarming like locusts."

Here again, we are about to be submersed in Nick's "flights of ideas" as he randomly associates locusts with grasshoppers and then distinguishes them from cicadas. Grasshoppers "become" locusts when they mass with other grasshoppers and swarm, but perhaps the most revealing similarity between all three—grasshoppers, locust and cicadas—is that they all go through an incomplete metamorphosis, exactly like Nick, who then warns his listeners:

> "You must not, however, make a confusion with the seven-year locust or cicada which emits a peculiar sustained sound which at the moment I cannot recall. I try to recall it but I cannot. I can almost hear it and then it is quite gone."[23]

Nick is alluding to the fact that he has very little control over what he thinks and therefore what he says and does. He is not in control of his own mind and has therefore "lost his marbles" or, put another way, he has what is commonly described as a "thought disorder."

The symptoms of **thought disorder** can include: (1) **paranoia**, often heightened by states of hypervigilance and defensive posturing; (2) **confusion** about the identity of the individual in his surroundings and false beliefs about others and their motivation (sometimes manifesting in anger and rage) and hearing or seeing non-describable events, things, or actions; and (3) disconnected thinking and speech resulting in language and expressions that are difficult to follow and understand, especially when the speaker switches quickly from one seemingly unrelated idea to another (sometimes called "**flights of ideas**"), or when the speaker rambles on in longwinded tangents of seemingly unrelated details and minutia that delay or sometimes entirely derail the speaker from ever reaching the point of the monologue (sometimes referred to as "**circumstantiality**"), or when the words used are illogically or inappropriately strung together resulting in gibberish (sometimes referred to as "**word salad**").

Nick would appear to present with all three of the above symptoms of thought disorder, in varying degree, as we shall see in striking detail as Hemingway pushes his character relentlessly onto the perilous precipice of chaos.

Before we look more closely at thought disorder(s) in "A Way You'll Never Be," another relevant aspect of PTSD is that it calls into question the difference between forgetfulness and amnesia. This is particularly germane to our story in that Nick clearly acknowledges his propensity not only to forget artifacts but—more importantly—to forget their spatiotemporal relationship(s) even when he can recall them to mind.

We suspect that Nick's received some sort of injury to his head severe enough that trepanning was considered but his doctors elected to let fluid be "re-absorbed." Nick could have sustained a traumatic brain injury, in which case his "forgetfulness" could be **neurological (organic) amnesia** caused by damage to the brain, specifically the hippocampus region. And we know, too, that being "nutty" for Nick is his obsession with trying to "get it right" in his recollections of the things in his past and his failure to do so on any sustained basis: his tests for "sameness" and repeatable results from persistent inquiry are—except in one case thus far—doomed to failure.

But Nick could just as likely be diagnosed with **psychogenic (functional) amnesia** caused by traumatic stress, intense fear, and witnessing or participating in particularly gruesome activities or events.

Whether or not Nick's degree of "forgetfulness" and his inability to recall certain people, places, things and events is related to a physical or a psychological cause, the end result is similar except for one very important distinction: **"self-induced" amnesia** in which the mind—to protect "itself" from going crazy and creating irreparable harm to the individual or to those around him—consciously clouds aspects of the past, shrouds them, or masks them entirely from review and therefore intrusion.

This creates a dynamic tension in individuals suffering from PTSD, especially when they get caught up in a tug-o-war of wanting desperately to remember and/or wanting just as desperately to forget, which in turn generates approach-avoidance and fight-or-flight battles that so many veterans experience every day and night of their lives.

"Why does my mind constantly torture me every fucking night by making me relive that same scene over and over again! What does **it** want of me? What is **it** trying to prove?" was an Iraqi War veteran's response when asked about a repetitive nightmare that had lasted for four years.[24] And yet, in his particular dream sequence, "**it**" couldn't remember what the nearly severed head and mangled face of his best buddy looked like when he rolled him over. Not only that, he couldn't remember what his buddy's face looked like prior to the ambush nor anything about his buddy's personal life: wife, children, where he grew up, etc. Here, the "**it**" could be perceived as both persecuting and defending.

For many veterans, some of these scenes remembered appear in distorted backgrounds, colors, sounds, smells and even tastes. Somehow the blood is redder, the explosions louder, the cries of the wounded more piercing, the odor of blood and urine more pungent as is the sandpaper grit of dust on your teeth and the taste of explosives. And yet for others, their internal "movies" are silent, sometimes seeing themselves as "audience" one minute, and "actor" the next. Even more important is the way in which the individual becomes a main character in his own internal drama. Many veterans, who describe themselves as characters in their nightmares, often see themselves in the third-person subjective. In that sense, they are the script writer, the producer, and the actor all in one. The degree of dissociation is critical here as some vets explain how they "join" with themselves in some scenes and "separate" from themselves in others, most often when the worst is about to happen or when they do something they feel is cowardly or less than honorable, in one case intentionally shooting civilians. In some scenarios, the memories transport the beholder to a safe haven one minute and to hell the next which is well beyond the benign, old adage that "memory is a faculty that forgets."[25] Rather, this is PTSD.

Back to the story: once Nick concludes his rambling remarks about grasshoppers and his inability to recall the sound of cicadas, he makes this statement to the adjutant:

"You will pardon me if I break off our conversation,"

at which point the adjutant orders one of the runners to see if he can find the major and then turns back to Nick:

"I can see you have been wounded."

This must come as yet another crushing blow to Nick's "identity" crisis: even the adjutant can "see" that Nick is "nutty."

The adjutant, having witnessed the nervous collapse of Nick's mental apparatus and seeing the rapid deterioration in Nick's condition is clearly concerned, perhaps even frightened, and motions with his hand to the second runner who presumably runs off to try to find Para as well.

After the runner departs, Nick continues to speak to the adjutant and some of the other troops at headquarters room and tells them to

> "Fix your eyes on the uniform. Spagnolini made it, you know. You might as well look, too," Nick said to the signalers. "I really have no rank. We're under the American consul."

If there is any doubt left in our minds that Nick has cobbled himself together and rendered pieces and parts of various uniforms and decorations into this patchwork of suspicious identity, then this admission seems to confirm that Nick is not in an American uniform, he has no rank, and is probably not in any army since he apparently operates under the control of the American consul. He is a wandering ragbag of memories, scenes, and reflections as he describes—in run-on manner—"the American locust," grasshoppers, and how to use them for bait and how to catch them, in great detail in lecture-like format, which he concludes with:

> "I hope I have made myself clear, gentleman. Are there any questions?"

The audience, no doubt stupefied and anxious by this time, have no questions, prompting Nick to conclude with:

> "Then I would like to close on this note. In the words of that great soldier and gentleman, Sir Henry Wilson: Gentlemen, either you must govern of be governed. . . . That is all, Gentlemen. Good day."

In Nick's instruction to "either govern or be governed," Hemingway is drawing from some of the political writings of Sir Henry Wilson, but also a slew of other political theorists who espouse the same notion, sometimes in a more aggressive tone like: "if you can't govern yourself, then we will," which is something left over from the Colonial Period. By Hemingway putting this notion in Nick's mouth, so to speak, Hemingway is also directly undermining and highlighting Nick's inability to govern himself.

Nick, who had put on his helmet shortly before this major thought-disorder episode, removes it and puts it on again and is apparently on his way out of the door just as Para returns with the two runners. As they meet at the entrance, Nick removes his helmet again and turns to Para:

> "There ought to be a system for wetting these things," he said. "I shall wet this one in the river." He started up the bank.

Paravicini calls after Nick:

> "Where are you going?"

To which Nick replies:

> "I don't really have to go." Nick came down the slope, holding the helmet in his hands. "They're a damned nuisance wet or dry. . . . You know they're absolutely no damned good," Nick said. "I remember when they were a comfort when we first had them, but I've seen them full of brains too many times."

Para, seeming to understand enough about Nick's plight to be helpful and concerned, takes over control of Nick, in essence fulfilling the role of "governing" that Nick clearly lacks at this time: Para tells Nick that he thinks Nick should go back.

But Para exercises his control in an amazingly sensitive, compassionate and clever way: he tells Nick that the reason that Nick needs to go back is to collect "those supplies" ("the chocolate, the postal cards, and cigarettes") required to "carry out his assignment." Then Para presses the issue further and enlists Nick's concern for the safety of his men:

> "If you move around, even with something worth giving away, the men will group and that invites shelling. I won't have it."

Nick responds in a manner that is at once a confession and a defensive plea:

> "I know it's silly," Nick said. "It wasn't my idea. I heard the brigade was here so I thought I would see you or someone else I knew."

Para ignores Nick's lame excuse for being back at battalion headquarters and repeats his request almost as a command:

> "I won't have you circulating around to no purpose."

This exchange between Nick and Para provokes another of Nick's "episodes," only this time Nick is well aware of the looming presence of something ("**it**"?) other than Para or himself taking control of his thoughts:

> "All right," said Nick. He felt **it** coming on again.
> "You understand?"
> "Of course," said Nick. He was trying to hold **it** in.
> "Anything of that sort should be done at night."

"Naturally," said Nick. He knew he could not stop **it** now.

"You see I am commanding the battalion," Para said.

"And why shouldn't you be?" Nick said. Here **it** came. "You can read and write, can't you?"

"Yes," said Para gently. [Emphasis mine.]

Para ignores Nick's comment and challenges Nick as to where he left his bicycle and then suggests that Nick lie down for a little bit, to which Nick agrees. But the instant he closes his eyes he's driven (by "**it**"?) headlong into a frightening scene in which the

> . . . man with the beard who looked at him over the sights of the rifle, quite calmly before squeezing off [a round], the white flash [from the muzzle] and clublike impact [of the round hitting him], on his knees, hot-sweet [blood] choking [him], coughing it [the blood] onto the rock while they [the enemy?] went past him . . . [Brackets mine.]

is replaced with another scene in which

> . . . he saw a long, yellow house with a low stable and the river much wider that it was and stiller.

Presumably, this may be that last "frame" Nick recalls prior to losing consciousness from being wounded. Had he not survived, it would have been the last image he saw before he died, and that is the terror embodied in the scene with the "long, yellow house with a low stable and the river."[26]

These two recollections—the "man with the beard" juxtaposed against the "yellow house"—have instantaneous and dramatic effects on Nick that converge to point him in a positive direction.

First, Nick makes a straightforward, purposeful decision: he's leaving now. He agrees with Para that he won't return until he has the "supplies" and that he'll "travel at night."

But Para, perhaps still concerned about Nick, cautions him:

"It is still hot to ride."

To which Nick, seemingly composed and on top of things, replies:

"You don't need to worry," Nick said. "I'm all right now for quite a while. I had one but then it was easy. They're getting much better. I can tell when I am going to have one because I talk so much."

This is a remarkably insightful milestone for Nick: although he may not know why these "spells" come over him, he at least acknowledges that they do happen and that he's even cognizant of their loquacious beginnings and circumloquacious endings in a manner not unlike how some veterans suffering from PTSD come calmly to these sudden moments of truth about themselves and their condition.

This level of self-awareness is the genesis of Nick's ability to retake control of himself again and suggests that he may have the ability to "work though" his condition and at least "come to an understanding" of why he has his problems. But most indicative of Nick's growing confidence is when he rejects Para's request that a runner accompany him: Nick knows he needs to try to find his own way back alone, by himself and for himself

"As a mark of confidence."

Many veterans who have experienced some sort of psychological trauma express this universal need to attempt to set and reach personal goals where he or she progressively regains confidence in their thoughts and actions. Trying to reach those levels of confidence can be frustrating, depressing, painful, exhausting, and even dangerous when constant failure or lack of support undermines every attempt.[26]

It's also incredibly complicated, as we've just witnessed in Hemingway's telling of a very short story about a young American wounded in Italy. Earning—or maybe I should say re-earning—the "mark of confidence" is a struggle common to all of us at varying points in our lives regardless of whether or not we've been physically or mentally "wounded" in combat. Gaining confidence and demonstrating that confidence to others is one of the single most important thresholds for suffers of PTSD to reach. It comes in small challenges and even smaller steps, often undermined by a lack of self-esteem, troubled personal relationships, drug and alcohol dependencies, inability to retain employment, unable to concentrate in academic and learning environments, eruptive and unpredictable emotional outbursts, run-ins with law enforcement, and homicidal and suicidal ideations. One vet plagued with some of these conditions and setbacks broke down crying and in two sentences summed it all up: "I'm so afraid. I have no ability. . . I have no idea how to raise my own son."[27]

Confidence. Confidence to raise a son. Sail a boat. Take the training wheels off. To enter into a relationship. To be hired. To pass an exam. To save a marriage. To make someone happy. To help a neighbor. To save a life, maybe your own.

Nick is at least confident enough to step up to the plate in front of Para. By turning down the offer of a runner, Nick is signaling his intent to try to make this one passage back to Fornaci successfully on his own. There's a lot at stake.

Para bids Nick "ciao," and Nick leaves and starts back "along the sunken road to where he had left the bicycle" and, seemingly unprovoked, Nick resumes his mental meanderings and recreates the visual artifacts that constitute his journey from present back into the past beginning with:

> . . . there were trees on both sides that had not been shelled at all. It was on that stretch that, marching, they had passed the Terza Sovia cavalry regiment riding in the snow with their lances. The horses' breath made plumes in the cold air. No, that was somewhere else. Where was that?

It would appear that the story is starting all over again, just with a different topology and set of artifacts and timelines; but this time Nick breaks the captivating, kidnapping influence of his randomly accessible memory and stream-of-conscious associations and forces himself to live in the here and now with a self-directed directive:

> "I'd better get to that damned bicycle," Nick said to himself. "I don't want to lose the way to Fornaci."

Let's hope Nick finds his way.

FOOTNOTES

1. Sher, L. (2004). Recognizing post-traumatic stress disorder. *QJM 97* (1): 1-5. doi:10.1093/qjmed/hch003
http://qjmed.oxfordjournals.org/content/97/1/1.2.long

2. Scholten JD, Sayer NA, Vanderploeg RD, Bidelspach DE, Cifu DX. (2012).Analysis of US Veterans Health Administration comprehensive evaluations for traumatic brain injury in Operation Enduring Freedom and Operation Iraqi Freedom Veterans. *Brain Inj. 26*(10): 1177-84. doi:10.3109/02699052.2012.661914. Epub 2012 May 30.

3. Hemingway, E. (2003). A Way You'll Never Be. In *The Nick Adams Stories*. (pp.154-167). New York: Scribner.

4. Hemingway describes the incoming mortar blast and psychic aura in a letter to a friend: "There was one of those big noises you sometimes hear at the front. I died then. I felt my soul or something coming right out of my body, like you'd pull a silk handkerchief out of a pocket by a corner. **It** flew around and then came back and went in again and I wasn't dead anymore." [Emphasis mine. More on the "it" later in this investigation.] Excerpt from *The Hemingway Resource Center*, Ernest Hemingway Biography.
http://www.lostgeneration.com/ww1.htm

5. "I have said that poetry is the spontaneous overflow of powerful feelings: it takes its origin from emotion recollected in tranquility: the emotion is contemplated till by a species of reaction the tranquility gradually disappears, and an emotion, kindred to that which was before the subject of contemplation, is gradually produced, and does itself actually exist in the mind." William Wordsworth, Preface to *Lyrical Ballads*.

6. When discussing this issue of **identity and confidence** with many veterans suffering from PTSD, almost all recounted specific incidents where a lack of confidence in their recollections undermined their sense of "self" before the precipitating traumatic event occurred as well as their "self" post-event. They see themselves as two different "selfs"—like the example of holding up two pictures of the same person which we can identify as the same person because of the degree of sameness—but who in fact are not exactly the same anymore. For those dealing with PTSD, maintaining that before-and-after appearance of sameness is an agonizing struggle to try to infuse the current self with the attributes of the past self lost forever in the shrouds of traumatic incidents in which the individual may have participated or witnessed or both. Notes and Observations: Interviews. 2000. Charles Coleman.

7. Ibid.

8. Griffin, Peter. *Along With Youth: Hemingway, The Early Years.* New York: Oxford University Press, 1985. 92. Print.

9. Ibid. Hemingway Resource Center. www.lostgeneration.com

10. When I've asked veterans who have told me that they suffer from horrendous bouts of "fear for their sanity" and why they don't seek help, most reply that they're even more fearful of being labeled "mental" and the stigma that comes with it. One vet went so far as to tell me that he drives to the VA once a week for OT for an injury he received on the battlefield, but never parks in the psych services parking lot even though that lot is significantly closer to his OT workout room, i.e. guilt by proximity and association. ("That lot's always empty.") This is an important subtlety: appearance is everything, and often what an individual

thinks of him/herself is more often dependant on the whims of the "viewing" public and the court of public opinion. ("Where you park is who you are. At least at this VA.") Notes and Observations: Interviews. 2004. Coleman.

11. Notes and Observations: Interviews. 2006 v3. Coleman.

12. Stevenson, Randall. *Modernist Fiction: An Introduction.* Lexington: University of Kentucky Press, 1992. 39.

13. Halbwachs, Maurice. (1950). Space and the Collective Memory In *The Collective Memory* (pp. 1-15). Retrieved from http://web.mit.edu/allanmc/www/hawlbachsspace.pdf

14. Dziuban, Z. (2012). Incorporating the Uncanny. *Das Unheimliche* as a Cultural Experience In Eds. Butler, S., Alves, F., Jaworski, K. *Madness in Plural Contexts: Crossing Borders, Linking Knowledge.* Inter-Disciplinary Press. Retrieved from http://www.inter-disciplinary.net/wp-content/uploads/2011/08/dzuibanmapaper.pdf

15. For those suffering from PTSD, the comings and goings of the degree of unhomeliness is critical to an understanding of just how psychological dis-placement begins and ends as memories take control of our psychological and sometimes our physiological beings. Often, we have no control over the **stressors**, those spontaneously generated triggers that transport us into another time, place, and space that is not the one in which we are actually existing at that moment.

16. Hysteria runs the gambit from diseases caused by the nomadic movement of the woman's uterus ("wandering womb"), to including sexual dysfunction ("female hysteria"), to a "split consciousness," to Freud's psychoanalytic theory that

attributed hysterical symptoms to the mind's attempt to protect the individual from psychically-generated anxiety and stress, to today's American Psychiatric Association's "denial of hysteria" as a clinical term (starting in 1980— ironically the same year that the APA recognized "post traumatic stress disorder")—and places the notion under "dissociative disorders" to include dissociative amnesia, fugue, identity disorder, and depersonalization disorder.

17. Webb. Thomas. (2006) 'Dottyville'—Craiglockhart War Hospital and shell-shock treatment in the First World War. *J R Soc Med 99*(7): 342–346.
<http:www.ncbi.nlm.nih.gov/pmc/articles/PMC1484566/>

18. Here we have ". . . a house and a long stable and a canal?" Prior to that we have: ". . . a low house painted yellow with willows all around it and a low stable and there was a canal . . . ." And ". . . but it frightened him especially when the boat lay there quietly in the willows on the canal . . . ." And ". . . a low house painted yellow. . . it frightened him. That house meant more than anything and every night he had it." And ". . . that long yellow house. . . ." And sometimes with a mention of "the river" and at other times the river is not included in the scene.

Furthermore, in one artifact, we have a boat; in another two, we have willows "all around" the house, and "the boat" lying "quietly in the willows;" in three of the four renditions, we have a canal; in two recollections we have "a stable," in one instance that stable is "long," in the other its "low;" in four of the five renderings we have "a house," in one scene, the house is a "low house painted yellow," in another, it's just "a house," in the third and fourth, it's "a low house painted yellow;" and in the fifth, it's "that long yellow house."

19. Hemingway scholar William Adair seems to think that Hemingway's observations of the Battle of Portogrande, which Hemingway described in a newspaper story in 1922 in which the "Austrians and Italians attacked and counter-attacked in waist deep swamp water," may have influenced Hemingway's later stories. Whether fact or fiction from the author's standpoint, the critical point is Nick's state of confusion and his confounding of what may or may not have been "real" from his perspective.

20. Notes and Observations. Interviews. 2002 v2. Coleman.

21. Coleman, C. 2004. Op. Cit.

22. Ibid

23. The oddity of the phrase "make a confusion" immediately draws our attention to it, as Hemingway surely intended, and we get another glimpse into the workings of Nick's thought processes, which he knows are also "confused." But by phrasing it such, Nick is suggesting that the conscious mind itself may actually be capable of intentionally creating confusion, as though it had "a mind of its own," like a mind inside of a mind: "I am of two minds."

24. Notes and Observations: Interviews. 2012 v1. Coleman.

25. Ferrarotti, Frances.*Time, Memory, and Society*. New York: Greenwood Publishing. 1990. 109.

26. Somewhat reminiscent of Hemingway's own reaction to his wounding on the Austro-Italian Front on July 8, 1918.

27. Notes and Observations: Interviews. 2011 v2. Coleman.

See also:

http://www.amazon.com/Sergeant-Back-Again-Anthology-Commentary/dp/0615441254/ref=sr_1_1?ie=UTF8&qid=1396107263&sr=8-1&keywords=sergeant+back+again+anthology

www.sergeantbackagain.com

ABOUT THE AUTHOR

"The Vietnam War Novel that Made PTSD Real!"
(Philip Beidler, Ph.D.)

Charles Coleman is the author of the universally-acclaimed portrayal of PTSD embodied in his Vietnam War-era cult classic, *Sergeant Back Again* (Harper & Row, 1980), re-released in 2010 in *Sergeant Back Again—The Anthology of Critical and Clinical Commentary*, which contains the first collection of published critical and clinical writings regarding the earliest characterizations and manifestations of combat-related PTSD using a Vietnam novel as the catalyst for investigation, discussion, and analysis.

In ***The Anthology***, six highly-respected scholars, historians, and psychiatrists "weigh in" on the social, political, and medical aspects and consequences of the emergence of post-traumatic stress disorder during the Vietnam War Era and later manifested in troops returning from Iraq and now Afghanistan. It also sheds light on the reasons behind the escalation of veteran suicides, divorces, spousal abuse, drug and alcohol addiction, and homelessness. As psychiatrist Harold Kudler, M.D, says in *The Anthology*: **"Psychiatry is still struggling to see beyond abstractions in order to find the patients it left behind and the real heart of darkness that defines psychological trauma."** http://www.sergeantbackagain.com/anthology.html)

Charles received his doctoral degree from SUNY Binghamton in 1977 for his Distinguished Dissertation—a graphic, psychological portrayal of combat-related post-traumatic stress syndrome/disorder among Vietnam War veterans published in 1980 under the title, *Sergeant Back Again*.

Charles is an author and lecturer on the subject of PTSD and is currently compiling a series of international use cases as an introduction to the universality of post-traumatic stress on and off the battlefield. He can be contacted through the *Sergeant Back Again* web site at www.sergeantbackagain.com or via email at dr.charles.coleman@gmail.com.

✚ ABOUT PTSD PRESS

PTSD PRESS was founded in 2010 to promote a greater awareness of the impact of post-traumatic stress experienced by individuals, communities, societies—indeed—civilizations who (which) have been traumatized by naturally-occurring or man-made events. Although originally chartered to focus on active-duty servicemen and veterans of wars, that charter has expanded to include both victims and—in the case of purposeful traumatic actions against another person or people—the perpetrators themselves, which is to say that anyone involved in a traumatic event can develop signs and symptoms of PTSD.

Around the world today, we see so many examples of people on both sides of conflict forever affected by violence, bloodshed, murder, wholesale kidnapping, rape, torture, destruction of family and home, and the collapse of anything we would even remotely call civilized. But all of these are the overt manifestations of conflicts within our inner selves and as we participate in, or witness or are victims of trauma and traumatic events, we ourselves become the embodiment of the disorder.

It is the mission of PTSD PRESS to provide a voice, a palette, a camera and a stage for displaying and interacting with the creative outcomes of the experience of PTSD regardless of origin or cause in hope that expression through literature, art, drama, screenplays, songs and recordings, film, and other media can help us to better understand the causes, effects, outcomes, and provide healing for individuals and communities trying to recover from post-traumatic stress.

Please feel free to contact PTSD PRESS by emailing us through the PTSD PRESS website. If you are interested in submitting your work for publication, please click on the "Author's Inquiry" tab at www.PTSDPRESS.com.

www.ingramcontent.com/pod-product-compliance
Lightning Source LLC
Chambersburg PA
CBHW060617030426

42337CB00018B/3084